Launch into Literacy

Foundation Book

Jane Medwell ◆ Maureen Lewis

Contents

UNIT•1

Writing to instruct

UNIT•2

Writing to entertain

Writing to express

Writing to report

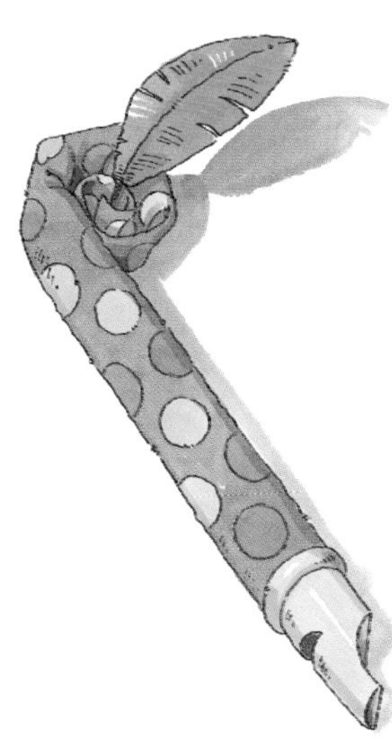

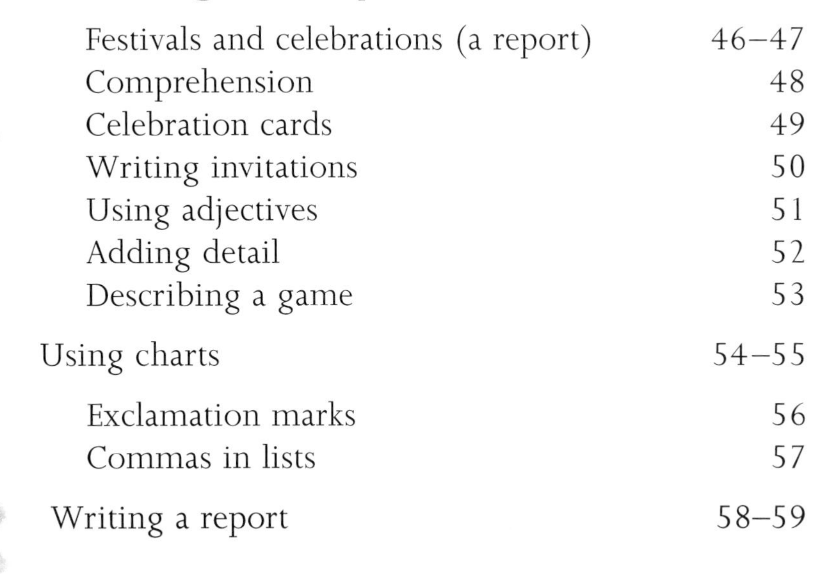

UNIT • 1

Writing to instruct

Instructions tell us how to do or make something.
In this unit you will study how instructions are written.
At the end of the unit you will write a set of instructions.

Instructions

- What is the aim of these instructions?
- Why is there a list of the things you need at the beginning?
- Why are the instructions given in order?
- Where did these instructions come from?
- Why were these instructions written?
- Who might read these instructions?

Text features: *aims, materials, steps*

How to make Marshmallow Treats

25 g	*butter or margarine*
40 g	*marshmallows*
50 g	***Kellogg's Rice Krispies***

- Melt the butter or margarine in a saucepan.
- Add the marshmallows and stir over a low heat until the marshmallows have melted and the mixture is well blended.
- Remove from the heat.
- Add the ***Kellogg's Rice Krispies*** and stir until well coated.
- Press the mixture into a greased 18 cm square tin.
- When cool cut into squares and then triangles.

CHILDREN: Whilst it can be great fun making Marshmallow Treats, a hot cooker can be dangerous! ALWAYS ASK AN ADULT TO HELP YOU IN THE KITCHEN.

Makes 18

aim

materials

precise information

technical words

commands

Reading skills: *comprehension*

Comprehension

1 Read the instructions 'How to make Marshmallow Treats'. Answer these **questions** about the passage.

a To make Marshmallow Treats you need
butter or margarine? *chocolate?* *milk?*

b You make Marshmallow Treats in
the oven? *a saucepan?* *the freezer?*

c The mixture is put into
a triangular tin? *a round tin?* *a square tin?*

d It is important to
use a high heat? *use no heat?*
use a low heat?

e How many Marshmallow Treats does the recipe make?

f Why do you need to have an adult with you when you make Marshmallow Treats?

Remember
You can use a dictionary to look up word meanings.

2 Now answer these questions about the words in the instructions.

a The word 'blended' means
mixed? *cooked?* *frozen?*

b The word 'coated' means
stuck together? *covered?* *hot?*

3 Make a list of the equipment you need to make Marshmallow Treats.

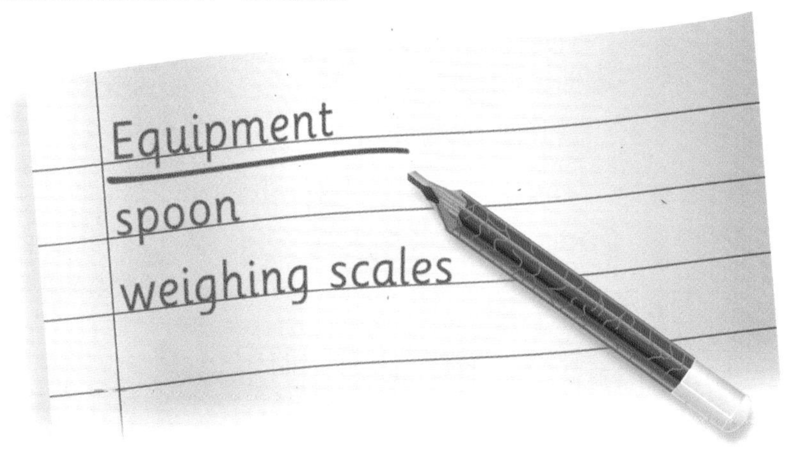

Glossary question

Reading skills: *chronological order*
Writing skills: *sequencing, labelling, listing*

Events in order

The recipe on page 5 tells you what to do in time order. This is called **chronological order**. It is important to get the order of instructions right.

Here is a set of instructions for making something to eat. The list is in the wrong order.

1 Write these instructions out in the correct order.

2 Write a **title** for the instructions.

Remember
The title must say what the aim of the instructions is.

3 Write a list of 'Things you will need' for this recipe. Include ingredients and equipment.

4 Copy out the **diagram** and add these **labels**.
a filling **b** bread **c** margarine

Glossary
title
label
diagram

Sentences

A **sentence** is a piece of writing which makes sense, starts with a **capital letter** and ends with a **full stop**, **question mark** or **exclamation mark**.

1 The words in these sentences are squashed up. Write them out with spaces in the right place.

a Puttheteabagintothecup.

b Pouronsomehotwater.

c Addmilktoyourtea.

2 The words in these sentences are muddled up. Write the sentences out with the words in the right order.

a into some the Pour kettle. water

b kettle. Switch on the

c the boils When off. turn kettle water the

3 Some of these groups of words are sentences. Write 'sentence' or 'not a sentence.'

a I like milk in my tea.

b Pour out the coffee.

c nice, hot chocolate

d I want orange juice.

4 How many sentences can you make using words from each of the mugs below?

Glossary
capital letter
full stop
question mark
exclamation mark

Capital letters and full stops

We mark **sentences** by beginning them with a **capital letter** and ending them with a **full stop**, **question mark** or **exclamation mark**.

1 Write the capital letters beside the small letters. The first one is done for you.

d *D* t ___ k ___ r ___ i ___

2 Write out the sentences putting capital letters at the beginning of the sentences and full stops at the end of sentences. The first one is done for you.

a we are having sausages for tea
We are having sausages for tea.

b the boy ate greedily

c sally loves jam tarts

3 The passage below has no full stops and capital letters, so it is hard to read. Write out the passage putting capital letters at the beginning of the sentences and full stops at the end of sentences.

Remember
The title is a sentence.

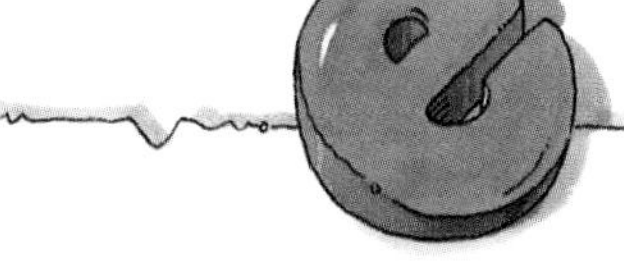

how to make tea

first you need to pour water in the kettle then boil the water put tea bags into the tea pot pour boiling water on the tea pour the tea into cups or mugs add milk and sugar if you like

Glossary
sentence
full stop
question mark
exclamation mark

UNIT·1 Writing to instruct

Grammar: *nouns*

Nouns – words that name

Words that name people, things or ideas are called **nouns**.

1 Write down the words you can use instead of the pictures in this passage. These words are nouns.

2 Write the labels for these pictures. All these words are nouns.

3 Most sentences contain nouns. Write out the sentences below. Instead of drawing the pictures write down nouns. The first one is done for you.

a The [picture] is sleeping. *The cat is sleeping.*

b The [picture] felt happy.

c What a huge [picture] !

d The [picture] ate the cheese.

4 Write down the nouns in these sentences. The first one is done for you.

a I love chocolate. *chocolate*

b The cat is black all over.

c The biscuit is soggy.

d A car is coming!

Glossary
label
sentence

Alphabetical order

Vocabulary: *alphabetical order*

Alphabetical order is the order of the letters in the alphabet.

1 Write the missing letters.

a a, b, ___, ___, e, f

b G, H, ___, ___, K, L

c r, s, ___, u, ___, w

2 Write the two letters that come next in alphabetical order.

a c, d, e, f, ___, ___,

b S, T, U, ___, ___,

c b, c, d, ___, ___,

3 Arrange the **nouns** in alphabetical order using the first letter of each word to decide the order.

EXAMPLE: cake, biscuit, sandwich
biscuit, cake, sandwich

a lemonade, coke, water

b tea, coffee, soup

c fig, apple, banana

4 The words in a dictionary are arranged in alphabetical order. Use the alphabet on this page to decide whether the words below are in the first half or the second half of the dictionary. Make two lists.
cup, pot, bowl, spoon, grater, whisk, glass

Remember
Use a dictionary to help you.

5 Write down a noun for each letter of the alphabet. The first three have been done for you.
apple, bowl, cat,

Glossary
noun

Writing directions

Dervla has drawn a sketch plan and written instructions for finding her school from the station.

Directions to get to Hope Street school from the station.

1 At the exit from the station go left.
2 Turn right by the traffic lights and walk along the road by the river.
3 Turn right and go over the bridge.
4 Walk straight on and you will go past the church.
5 Go through the park past the pond on your left.
6 Keep walking until you arrive at the school.

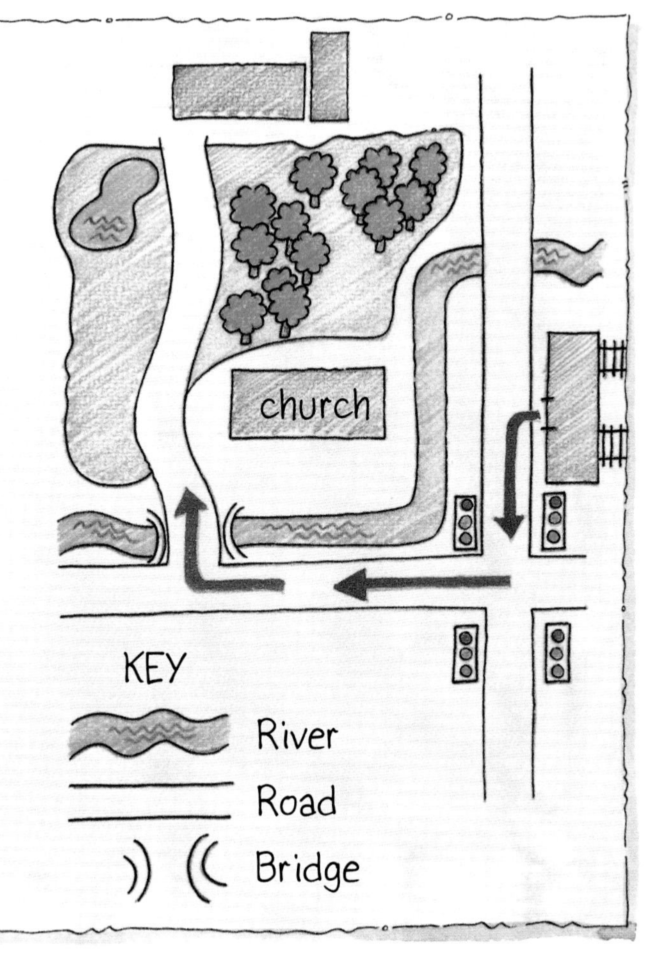

1 Dervla has labelled the church. Use her instructions to follow the route and name the other landmarks.

2 Imagine you are following the route on the map. After crossing the bridge, which do you pass first?
a pond? *some trees?* *a church?*

3 Is each of these landmarks on your left or right?
a church **b** trees **c** pond

4 Draw a sketch plan of your classroom and **label** some things a stranger would see.

Text features: *labelling, listing*
Reading skills: *reading for detail*
Grammar: *prepositions*

Words for places

Dervla's directions used **prepositions** – words that tell you about place.

over in behind
above around
on by
under along down

1 Write out these **sentences** with prepositions.
 a The cow jumped ______ the moon.
 b Jack and Jill fell ______ the hill.
 c Boys and girls come ______ to play.
 d Humpty Dumpty sat ______ a wall.

2 Imagine you are walking from your school entrance to your class. Answer these **questions**.
 a What do you walk across?
 b What doors do you go through?
 c What buildings or trees do you walk past?
 d What do you walk under?

3 Draw a sketch plan from your school entrance to your classroom. **Label** the landmarks.

4 Now write the directions. Make sure you use sentences and prepositions.

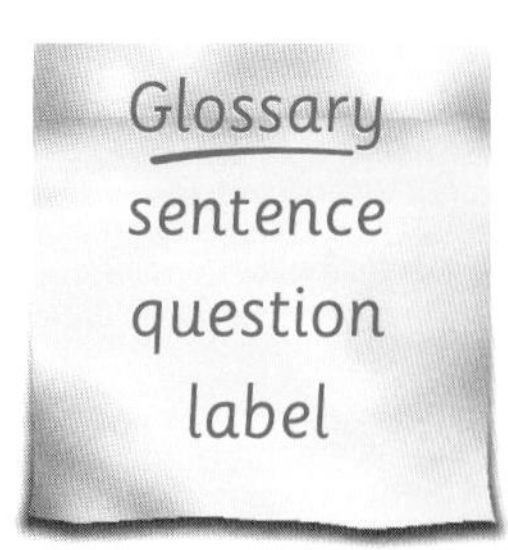

Verbs

Most sentences contain a **verb**. A verb is a word which says what a person is doing or being.
EXAMPLE: Dervla **runs** along the street.
'**runs**' is a verb.

1 Write down what these children are doing.

2 Most sentences contain a verb. Put the verb into each sentence so that it makes sense.

a Minnie ________ along the road.
b Then she ________ down the hill.
c Finally she ________ into the wall.

3 Write down the verbs in these sentences.
a Mum walks quickly.
b Baby David crawls along.
c Dad jogs in the morning.
d Sally skates to school.

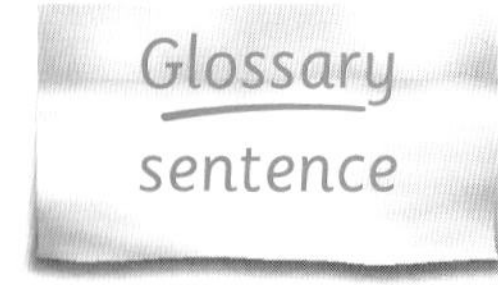

Grammar: *imperative sentences*

Commands

Some sentences are **commands**. They tell us what to do. These are called **imperative sentences**.

1 Some of the sentences below are commands (imperatives) and some are not. Write 'command' or 'not command' for each sentence.

a The cat is black.
b Catch the cat.
c Go to bed.
d I am very tired.
e Drink some milk.
f Here is a bun.

2 Read these sentences.

He walks through the park.
Walk through the park.

The second sentence is a command. It tells the reader what to do. Change sentences **a** to **c** into commands. EXAMPLE: She runs to the shop.
Run to the shop.

a They eat breakfast quickly.
b I pick up the mess.
c She jumps off the wall.

3 What do these signs tell you to do? Write a command for each sign.

Glossary
sentence

Writing instructions

You have seen that instructions tell the reader how to do something. You are going to write a set of instructions which tell the reader how to play a simple game.

1 Choose a simple game you know well, e.g. noughts and crosses, hangman, jacks or hopscotch. Discuss it with a friend and write down some important words as a brainstorm web.

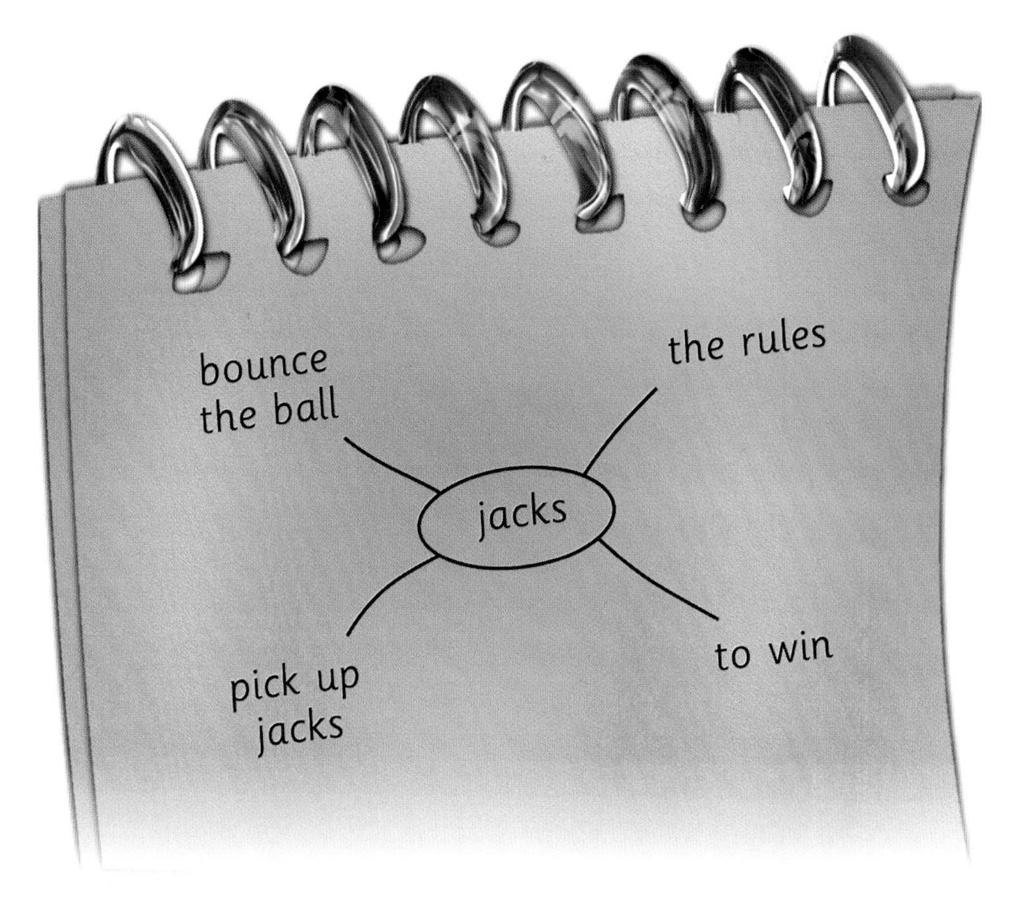

2 Think about what you need to tell someone who does not know the game. Answer these questions.

a What do you do to win the game?
b How many people play the game?
c What equipment do you need?
d What do you do to play the game?

3 Write a title for your instructions.

4 Write a draft of your instructions.
Use these headings:
- Title
- The aim of the game
- Things you need to play
- What to do

5 Draw a diagram of the things you use to play the game and label it.

6 Read your instructions to a friend.
- Is it clear what you have to do to win?
- Do the instructions tell you exactly what to do?
- Do the instructions tell you how many people can play?
- Can your friend understand what to do?
- Are your instructions in sentences with capital letters and full stops?

7 Rewrite your draft very clearly.

UNIT • 2

Writing to entertain

In this unit you will study the way stories are written. At the end of the unit you will plan, draft and revise your own story.

The Hurricane Tree

Once upon a time there was a boy called William, who lived in an old house underneath a tall tree.

In the spring, the tree was like a big pale green umbrella, higher than the rooftop, and if William looked into the branches, he could see birds building their nests.

In the summer, he had his lunch under the tree, then leaned on its smooth warm trunk and fed the crumbs to the squirrels.

Does this sentence catch your interest?

setting refers to an old house underneath a tree

main character

Text features:
story, character, setting, time

Beginning a story

Look at how the author begins the story so that it will be interesting.

In the autumn, the tree dropped sticky prickly beech nuts into William's sandpit, and threw down heaps of dry golden leaves. He made beds out of them and mountains and kicked them into snowstorms.

And in the winter, when the real snow came, his mummy sometimes took him to the kitchen window at bedtime, to see the big yellow moon at the top of the tree. "It looks like a balloon tangled up in the branches," said William. "One day, when I'm big, I'm going to climb right up that tree and sit next to the bird's nest and look at the stars."

clue to what will happen

by L. Purves

Character and settings

1 Reread the passage from *The Hurricane Tree* on pages 18 and 19.

2 Write the answers to these **questions**.

a The author of the story
wrote the story? drew the pictures? printed the book?

b The illustrator
wrote the story? drew the pictures? printed the book?

c The main character is
a boy called William? a squirrel? a bird?

d 'tangled' means
behind? caught in? floating in?

e List two animals which use the tree.

f Where is the setting for the story?

g How old do you think William might be?

Glossary question

Months and seasons

Reading skills: *comprehension*
Vocabulary: *months and seasons*

1 Write out these months in the right order.
  a The months of spring are May, April and March.
  b The months of summer are July, June and August.
  c The months of autumn are September, November and October.
  d The months of winter are February, January and December.

2 Read this **rhyme** aloud to a friend and learn it.

Thirty days has September,
April, June and November.
All the rest have thirty-one,
Except for February alone
Which has twenty-eight days clear.
And twenty-nine each leap year.

Remember
The names of months begin with a capital letter.

3 Write out these **sentences**, filling the blanks.
  a June has ______ days.
  b August has ______ days.
  c September has ______ days.

4 Which month doesn't always have the same number of days?

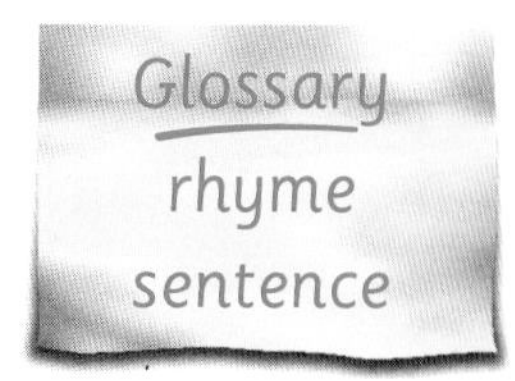

Grammar: *adjectives*

Adjectives – describing words

Adjectives are words that describe **nouns** in a sentence.

1 All colour words are adjectives. Write down the colours which you think describe each season.
EXAMPLE: winter *white, black, blue*
a spring **b** summer **c** autumn

2 Write out the colour adjective which is missing from each **sentence**.

a The ______ boat is sinking.
b The ______ bird is flying away.
c The ______ goat is eating the ______ dress.
d The ______ mouse is hiding.

3 Use an adjective and a noun from each list below to write a sentence each about spring, summer, autumn and winter.
EXAMPLE: *In winter the ground is white with snow.*

nouns:
leaves trees
sky ground

adjectives:
white yellow
blue orange
green

Glossary
noun
sentence

Writing skills/ composition: *similes*

Descriptions

One way to describe something is to compare it with something else. EXAMPLE: He is as strong as superman. This is called a **simile**.

1 In the passage from *The Hurricane Tree* on page 18 the author uses a simile to describe the tree: 'In the spring the tree was like a big pale green umbrella.' Make up similes to describe what the tree was like in the other seasons.

spring

summer

autumn

winter

a In the summer the tree was like ______.
b In the autumn the tree was like ______.
c In the winter the tree was like ______.

2 Here are some **sentences** that use **adjectives** and similes, but they don't quite make sense. Choose new adjectives so that the similes make sense.
EXAMPLE: The man was as small as a giant.
The man was as huge as a giant.
a The doll was as big as a mouse.
b The cat was as white as night.
c The leaf was as blue as grass.

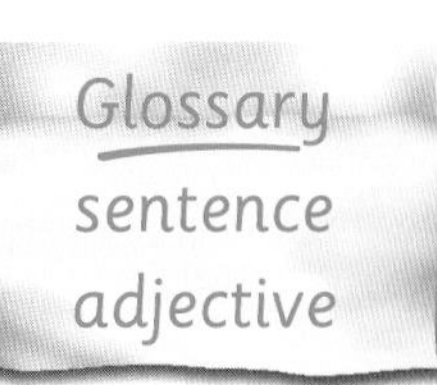

Verbs in stories

Words that tell us what is being done in a sentence are called **verbs**.
EXAMPLE: In hot weather Sally **drinks** lots of water.

1 Match each noun to a verb. Write out the sentences you make. The first one is done for you.

Nouns	Verbs
The bird	blows
The sun	grows
The rain	shines
The grass	flies
The wind	falls

The bird flies.

2 Write out the verbs in this poem. The first one is underlined for you.

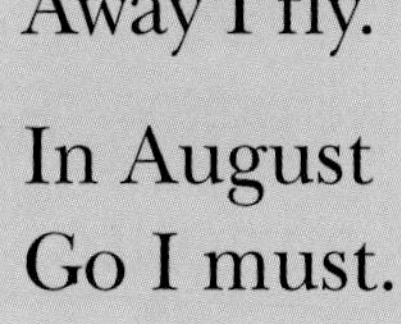

The Cuckoo

Cuckoo, cuckoo,
What do you <u>do</u>?

In April
I open my bill.

In May
I sing night and day.

In June
I change my tune.

In July
Away I fly.

In August
Go I must.

Anon

Glossary
sentence
noun

Grammar:
Past and present tense verbs

Tenses

The **tense** of a **verb** tells us when something is happening – now (the present), in the past or in the future.

1 Write down which of these events is happening in the present.
  a The cat is getting wet.
  b The sun shone yesterday.
  c The sun shines.

2 Change the verbs so that these **sentences** happened in the past. EXAMPLE: The dog jumps in the river.
The dog jumped in the river.
  a Sam shivers with cold.
  b Sally runs to get home.
  c The rain soaks the football players.

3 Sort these verbs into two lists – present tense and past tense.
- walk
- thought
- hop
- blew
- walked
- blow
- hopped
- think

Glossary
verb
sentence

Fiction and non-fiction

Fiction books tell you stories which have not really happened. **Non-fiction** books give you factual information. Fiction and non-fiction books use different types of words and pictures.

The Wind and the Sun

One day the wind and the sun argued about who was stronger.

"I am stronger than you," said the wind to the sun.

"Let us have a test to find out who is strongest," said the sun.

Then they saw a traveller walking along the road. They agreed that whoever could get the traveller to remove his coat was strongest. First the wind blew fiercely but the man wrapped his coat tightly round his body saying, "Brrr, it is so cold in this wind." Then the sun shone warmly until the man got so hot that he took off his coat.

1 Read the above pages. They are from two different books.

Types of winc

gale

2 Write the answers to these **questions**.

a List three words for types of wind.

b The fiction book is called
The Wind and the Sun? The Weather? How to Forecast Weather?

c The Beaufort Scale
tells a story? says how winds are caused? tells us about different wind strengths?

Glossary question

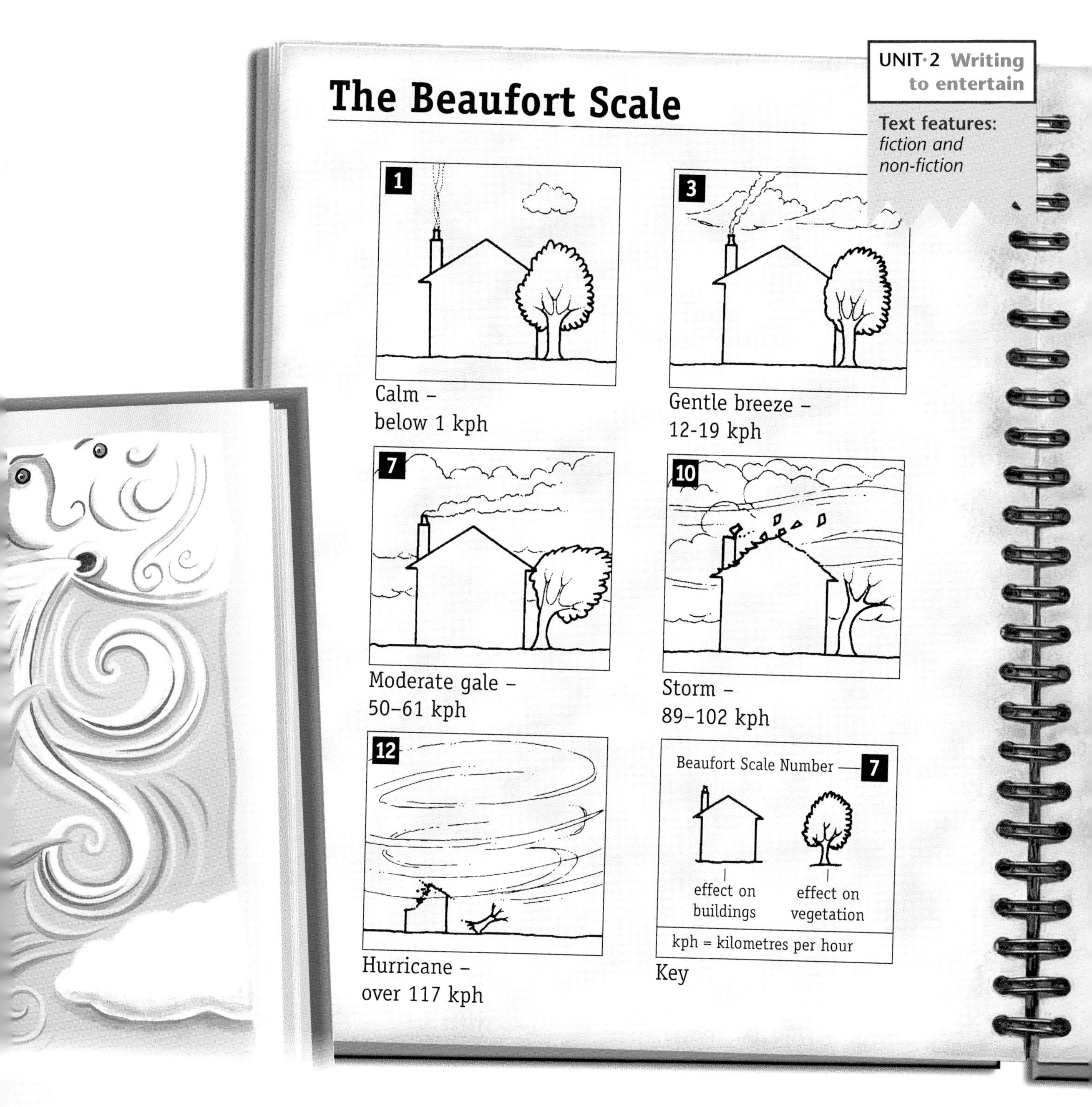

3 Look at the pictures on the pages above and answer these questions.

a What kind of illustrations does the Beaufort Scale have?

cartoons? *pictures?* *diagrams?*

b A **diagram** has **labels** because the labels

look nice? *add detail?* *don't fit the picture?*

c How do you know that 'The Wind and the Sun' is fiction?

Glossary
diagram
label

Text features: *chronological order*
Words: *homophones*

Time order

Instructions are always written in time order, which is called **chronological order**. In stories the events are also usually written in chronological order.

1 These pictures tell the story of 'The Wind and the Sun' but they are in the wrong chronological order. Re-order the letters to put the pictures in the right chronological order.

2 Write a sentence describing what is happening in each picture. These are the events.

Homophones

Some words have the same sound but different meanings and spellings. These are **homophones**.

1 Say these words out loud and try to think of the two meanings for each word.
bean/been blew/blue sun/son

2 Write out a sentence for each word to show the different meanings.

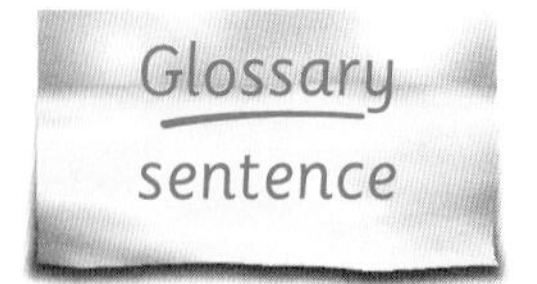

Characters speaking

Text features: *direct speech*
Punctuation: *speech marks*

The people in a story are known as the characters. We often learn about characters through what they say. This is called **direct speech**.

1 Draw a picture for each of the sentences below. Write what the character says in a speech bubble.
a "I am too hot," said Manny.
b Sanjay said, "I love the snow."
c Jane said, "I like the autumn leaves."

2 Read the story on page 26 again. Write exactly what the sun, the wind and the man say in each one of the three speech bubbles (**a**, **b**, **c**).

When we want to write down speech we use **speech marks** around what is actually said and any **punctuation** that goes with it, like **full stops**, **question marks** and **exclamation marks**.

3 Fill in the sentences below. Put the words that the sun, the wind and the man actually said inside the speech marks.
a "________," said the wind.
b The sun said, "________."
c The man said, "________."

Glossary
punctuation
full stop
question mark
exclamation mark

Writing a story

You are going to write a story. To do this you will need to think about the character, setting and events in a story.

1 Here are some pictures which can be arranged to make a story. Write down the order in which you think the pictures should go.

Character

2 Now write a sentence to say what is happening in each picture. These will be the events in your story. Here are some more pictures of the character in the story.

3 Choose a name for the main character and write a detailed description.

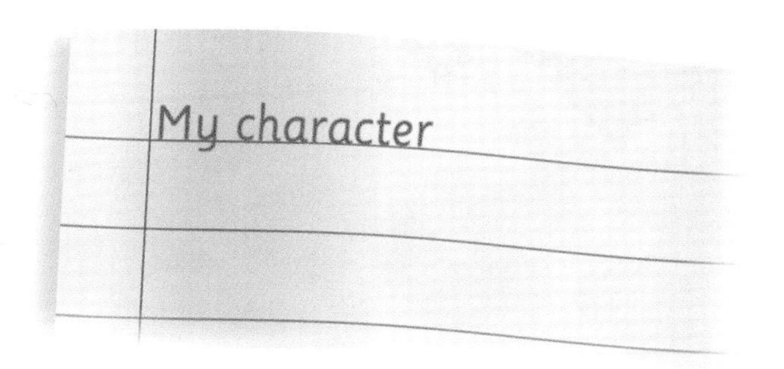

4 In your story the main setting is the park. Discuss these questions with a friend.
- What is in the park?
- What is the boy doing in the park?

Now write a detailed description of the setting.

5 Make a plan of what happens at the beginning, middle and end of the story.

6 Now you have the events of your story, a description of your character and a description of the setting. It is time to put all of your ideas together and write a draft of the story. Put in plenty of details so that the reader will find your story interesting and easy to imagine. Use one of these beginnings
- Once upon a time …
- One day …
- ________ was a stubborn boy.
- One sunny day …

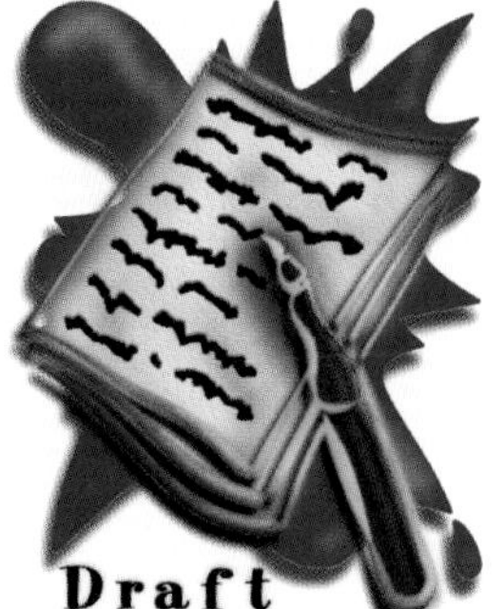

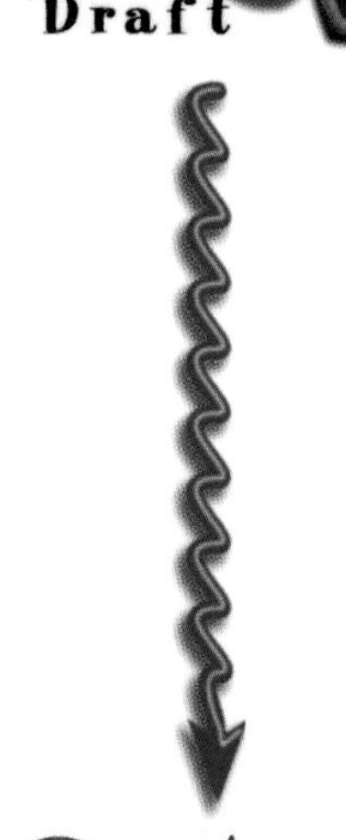

7 Swap your draft with a friend. Discuss these questions.
- Are the characters and setting easy to imagine?
- How could you make your story even better?

8 Mark any changes you want to make on the draft. Check any spellings you are not sure about.

9 Write out your story.

Writing to express

In this unit you will learn about rhyming poems. You will look at different ways to use rhyme and rhythm. At the end of the unit you will plan, draft and write your own funny, rhyming verse for a poem.

Funny poems

Some poems are funny because they talk about silly things.

- What is the poem opposite about?
- Do all the lines rhyme?
- Why does each verse begin the way it does?
- Why does each verse end the way it does?
- Does the poem have a rhythm when you read it aloud?

Text features: *rhyme, rhythm*

Did You Really?

Dip, dip, dip!
Did you ever lick
a lollipop stick
dipped into the mustard?
Did it make you sick?

My, my, my!
Did you ever try
a popcorn pie
chopped up with an onion?
Did it make you cry?

Hoo, hoo, hoo!
Did you ever chew
a bubble-gum stew
mixed up with custard?
Can I have some too?

by *Judith Nicholls*

How do these opening lines catch your interest?

What is a popcorn pie?

The last word of some lines rhyme

Is there a pattern of punctuation marks?

The Custard Company

Reading skills: *comprehension*
Vocabulary: *pairings, rhymes*

Using words

1 Read the poem 'Did You Really ?' on page 33 again. Fill in the missing words to complete the **sentences**.

a The lollipop stick was dipped into ____________.

b The onion was chopped with a ____________.

c The poet would like to eat some ____________.

2 Here are some more mixed up foods. Can you sort them out into sensible food pairs ?

Remember
You might jumble up things to write your own silly poem.

3 Think of two more pairs of food. Jumble them up to make silly foods. Draw and **label** them.

There are many words in the poem that **rhyme**. The ends of words which rhyme sound the same when we say them.
EXAMPLES: try/pie lick/stick

4 Add some more rhyming words to the lists. There are more words in the poem and you can add any others you know.

Glossary
sentence
label

Verbs

The poem on page 33 uses different eating verbs.
Here are some **verbs** for eating and drinking.

licked chewed nibbled sucked gobbled

1 Fill in the **sentences** below using these verbs.
At the harvest dinner everyone ate and drank well.
Leo ______ his drink through a straw. Jim was so hungry he ______ his food quickly. Sally ______ her sticky pudding for a long time.
Even a tiny mouse ______ some corn.

'a' or 'an'

The highlighted letters are all vowels. If a **noun** begins with a **vowel** it has an in front of it.
If a noun begins with a **consonant** it has a in front of it.

a b c d e f g h i j k l m n o p q r s t u v w x y z

2 Put 'a' or 'an' in the spaces.
a There was ___ old woman who lived in ___ shoe.
b My granny's basket holds ___ apple and ___ orange.

Glossary
verb
sentence
noun
vowel
consonant

Grammar: *direct speech*

Speech in bubbles

This poem starts like a well-known nursery **rhyme**. Changing something we know well can make it funny.

by Colin McNaughton

1 In the poem both the giant and the old woman speak. Write down what should go in each of the speech bubbles.

2 Write out what should go in the cat's speech bubble and in the kittens' speech bubble.

Three little kittens they lost their mittens,
And they began to cry,
"Oh, mother dear, we sadly fear
that we have lost our mittens."
"What! Lost your mittens?
You naughty kittens!
Then you shall have no pie."

Glossary
rhyme

Text features: *rhyming couplets*
Grammar: *verbs*

Rhyming couplets

Jump or Jiggle

Frogs jump
Caterpillars hump

Worms wiggle
Bugs jiggle

Rabbits hop
Horses clop

Snakes slide
Seagulls glide

Mice creep
Deer leap

Puppies bounce
Kittens pounce

Lions stalk
But –
I walk!

by Evelyn Beyer

This poem is written in pairs of lines. Each pair of lines **rhymes**. This is called a **rhyming couplet**. Here is a rhyming couplet about a person.

There was a boy called Sam
He liked bread and jam.

1 Use a name to make up a rhyming couplet.
There was a boy called ______. *He liked* ______.
or *There was a girl called* ______. *She liked* ______.

2 Now make up a rhyming couplet about a friend.

3 Make a list of the movement **verbs** from the poem.

4 Make up some more **sentences** using a different movement verb in each sentence.

Glossary
rhyme
verb
sentence

Question poems

Here are two more poems that use **rhyming couplets**. Both of these poems have a punch-line – an ending which makes the joke clearer.

Can you see the rhyme pattern?

How does the last line change the poem?

Shirley Said

Who wrote 'kick me' on my back?
Who put a spider in my mac?
Who's the one who pulls my hair?
Tries to trip me everywhere?
Who runs up to me and strikes me?
That boy there –
I think he likes me.

by Dennis Doyle

1 Answer these questions about the two poems.

a What does the boy do to Shirley's hair?
pull it? put a spider in it? comb it?

b Shirley thinks the boy
hates her? wants to go on a trip with her? likes her?

c A hog is another name for
a cat? a pig? a cow?

d Ducks, hens and geese are all
animals? insects? birds?

Glossary
rhyming couplet
rhyme

Questions end with a question mark.

when? what? why? how?
who? which? where?

are all question words that can begin questions.

UNIT 3 Writing to express

Text features: *rhyme patterns*
Reading skills: *comprehension*
Vocabulary: *question words*
Punctuation: *question marks*

The Answers

When did the world begin and how?
I asked a lamb, a goat, a cow.
What's it all about and why?
I asked a hog as he went by
Where will the whole thing end
and when?
I asked a duck, a goose, a hen.
And I copied all the answers too,
A quack, a honk, an oink and a moo.

by Robert Clairmont

Is there a rhythm if you read these aloud?

What punctuation mark tells you some of the sentences are questions?

2 List the six question words used in the two poems.

3 Think of two questions you would ask the cow in the poem above. Begin your sentence with one of the question words. End it with a question mark.

4 Think of two questions you would ask Shirley. Begin your sentence with one of the question words. End it with a question mark.

5 Make up an answer to one of your questions.

Glossary
question
question mark

Noisy words

The poem 'The Answers' on page 39 mentions the noises the animals make. The special noise words help us to build up a picture in our minds.

quack oink honk moo

1 Match the noises to the animals and birds.

hen	howl
dog	neigh
cat	sing
horse	baa
sheep	purr
blackbird	bark
wolf	cluck

Other noise words can sound like the sound they are describing when we say them aloud. The way we write them can also help us build a picture in our minds. EXAMPLE: SLURP!

Remember

We can use sound words in poems to help create a picture.

2 Say these noise words out loud. What does each one make you think of?
pow, chomp, ping, splat

3 Design your own way of writing these words.

What nonsense!

These two poems are funny because they put opposite ideas together.

One fine day in the middle of the night,
Two dead men got up to fight,
Back to back they faced each other,
Drew their swords and shot each other.

Anon

I went to the pictures tomorrow.
I took a front seat at the back.
I fell from the pit to the gallery,
And broke a front bone in my back.
A lady she gave me some chocolate.
I ate it and gave it her back.
I phoned for a taxi and walked it,
And that's why I never came back.

Anon

1 The first poem says they 'Drew their swords and shot each other'. Write silly endings for these lines.

a They waved their ties and ______.

b They took off their shoes and ______.

c They sharpened their pencils and ______.

2 The second poem says 'I went to the pictures tomorrow'. Why is this wrong?

Here are some more time words.

today **last night** **tomorrow** **last year**

3 Use the time words above to complete these **sentences**.

a ______ I am at school.

b I am one year older than I was ______.

c ______ I watched television.

d I am going to the cinema ______.

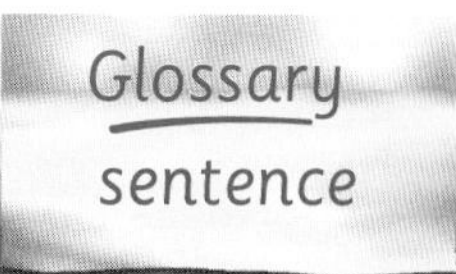

Vocabulary: *homographs, shortened words*

The same but different

The word 'back' is used to mean different things in the poems on page 41.

my back = a part of your body
at the back = a place in a room or crowd
give back = to return something

Words which are spelt the same but can have different meaning are called **homographs**.

Q Where do snowmen dance?
A At a snowball

Q When are sheep like ink?
A When they're put in a pen

Q Why are cooks bullies?
A They whip the cream and beat the eggs

1 Use each word in two sentences to show different meanings.

nail train spring flat bark

2 Read the poem 'I went to the pictures tomorrow' on page 41. Find these words in the poem:

a taxi **b** phone **c** pictures

Each of these words was once longer.

taxi cab telephone picture house

3 What is the short word we use for these words nowadays?

a 'aeroplane' is now _______.
b 'omnibus' is now _______.
c 'wellington boots' are now _______.
d 'refrigerator' is now _______.

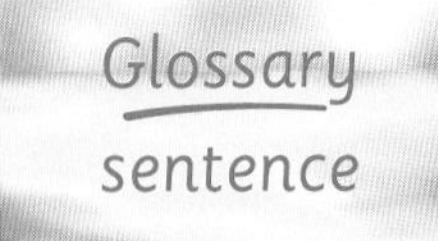

Grammar: *place names, capital letters*

Limericks

Limericks are five-line poems that all have the same **rhyme** pattern. They all have a strong **rhythm** too.

There was a young lady from Spain
Who hurried to catch the last train.
She shouted "Oh no!"
As she saw the train go.
"I'll have to walk home in the rain."

A greedy old man from Dundee
Liked ice cream and cakes for his tea.
He ate lots of jam
With bananas and ham
From a plate that he held on his knee.

1 Can you work out which place these people are from?
Use the rhyme to help you.

a A jolly lady from ______
Had a collection of snails.

b A girl from the Isle of ______
Gave her mother a fright.

c The skinny ballerina from ______
Said she had always wanted to dance.

2 Write a limerick using a place you know.
A ______ ______ from ______

Glossary
rhyme
rhythm

Writing a funny verse

You are now going to write your own silly rhyming verses to add to a well-known nursery rhyme.

Here are just a few verses from 'Old Mother Hubbard'. There are other verses. They all have the same rhythm and rhyme pattern.

Old Mother Hubbard

Old Mother Hubbard
Went to the cupboard
To get her poor dog a bone
But when she got there
The cupboard was bare
And so the poor dog had none.

She went to the bakers
To get him some bread
But when she came back
The poor dog was dead.

She went to the fruiters
To get him some fruit
But when she came back
He was playing the flute.

She went to the barbers
To buy him a wig
But when she came back
He was dancing a jig.

1 Brainstorm lots of different shops.

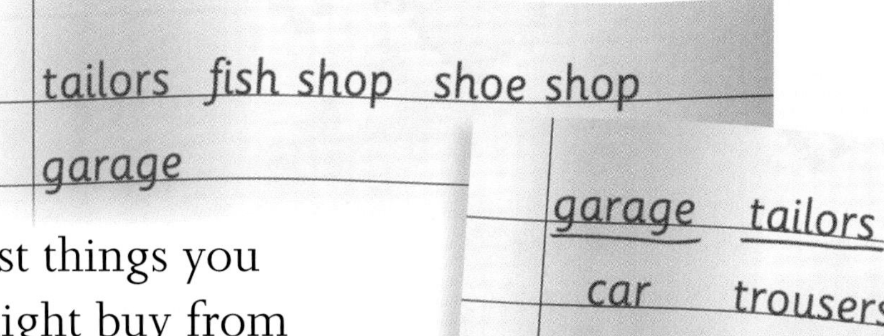

2 List things you might buy from two of these shops.

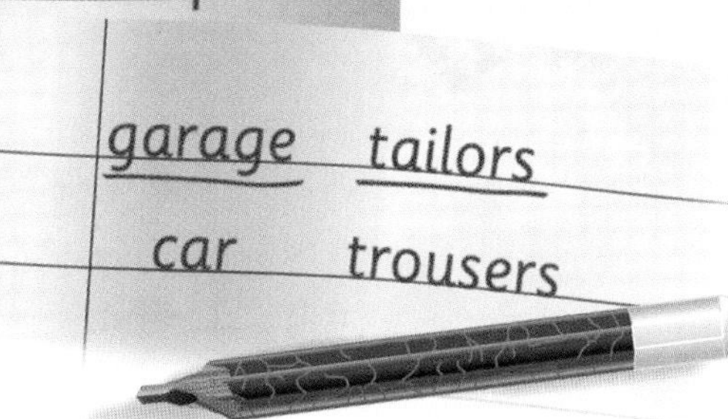

3 Think of rhyming words for things you've listed.

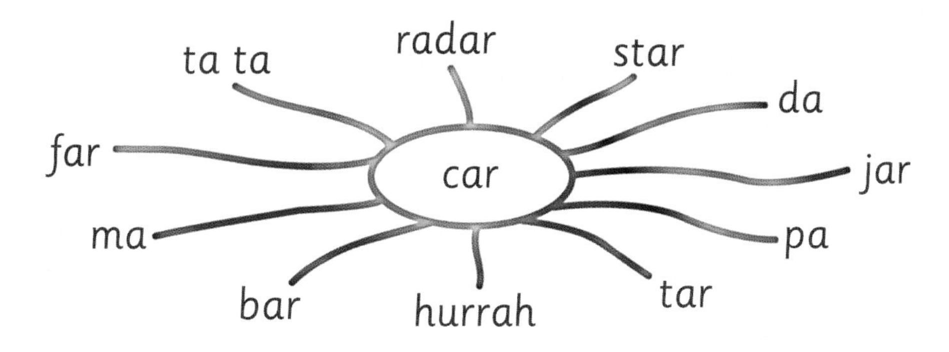

4 Use the words you have listed to write another verse for 'Old Mother Hubbard'.

EXAMPLE: She went to the garage
To buy him a car
But when she came back
He was shouting "Hurrah!"

5 Try one or two different ideas.

6 Discuss your ideas with a friend.
- Is it funny ?
- Does it rhyme in the correct places ?
- Have you used an interesting verb to describe what the dog was doing ?
- Have you used all the necessary punctuation ?

7 Make your own class version of 'Old Mother Hubbard'. You could produce a zigzag book with illustrations.

Writing to report

In this unit you will look at how we write reports. Reports tells us what things are. They describe what something is. At the end of the unit you will write your own report describing a special day.

Festivals and Celebrations

An opening definition

Festivals and celebrations are special events which mark important days. During celebrations people often wear special clothes, eat special foods and give each other cards and presents. Sometimes they decorate their houses too.

Details of what people do at festival time

There are festivals for important days in people's lives like birthdays, weddings and anniversaries.

8

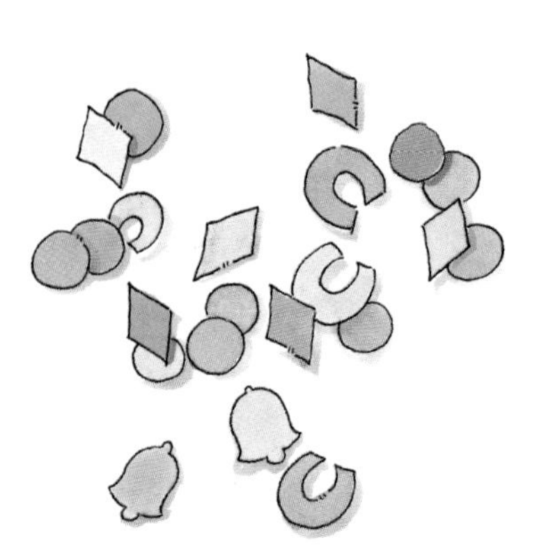

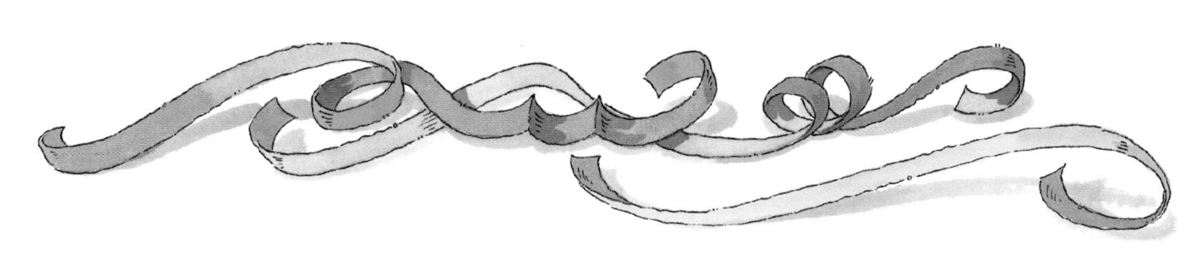

- What does the title of the report tell us?
- Why are there different parts to the report?
- Why are there photographs and captions?

There are special celebrations to mark important times of the year like harvest and New Year.

Chinese New Year celebrations

There are religious celebrations such as Christmas, Divali, Hanuka and Eid-Ul-Fitr. These special days remind people of important times in their religions.

Thanksgiving Day dinner

There are also special days to remind people of the important things that happened in their country like Thanksgiving Day in America and Independence Day in India.

9

More details in the photographs

Details of different kinds of festivals

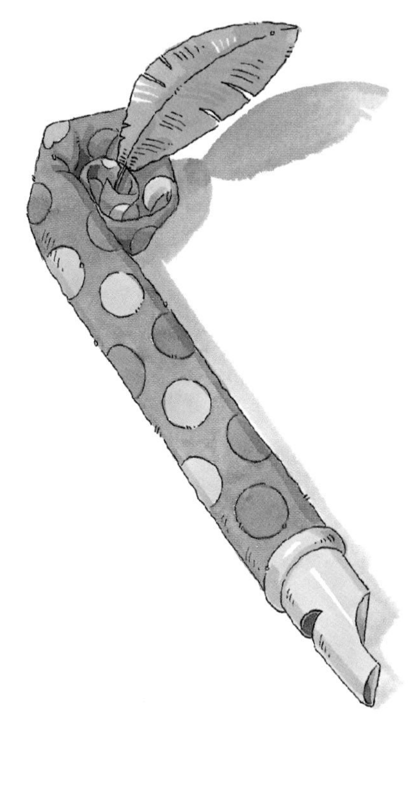

UNIT 4 Writing to report

Reading skills: *comprehension*
Grammar: *the verb 'to be'*

Comprehension

1 Read the report 'Festivals and Celebrations' on page 46 and 47, again. Remember to look at the pictures too. Fill in the missing words to complete the **sentences**.

a Christmas and Divali are times when people send ______

b Independence Day is celebrated in ______

c The photograph shows people eating a special meal on ______

d Birthdays and weddings are ______

The report on festivals uses the words 'there are' to start some sentences. 'are' is part of the **verb** 'to be'. The verb 'to be' is a very important verb in English.

2 Copy out and complete this chart of the verb 'to be'.

singular	plural
I am	we ______
you ______	you are
he, ______ or it ______	they are

Remember
Use the chart of the verb 'to be'.

3 Write out the following sentences. Circle the verb 'to be' in each of the sentences.

a I am having a birthday party today.
b It is my seventh birthday.
c My friends are all sending me cards.
d You are my friend.

Glossary
sentence
verb

Reading skills: *interpreting visual information*

Vocabulary: *days of the week*

Celebration cards

1 People send each other cards to mark special days. What special event do you think each of the cards below is for?

a ______ **b** ______ **c** ______

2 Read the poem 'Solomon Grundy'. Write down which day of the week should go under each of the cards for Solomon Grundy.

a ______ **b** ______ **c** ______

a

Solomon Grundy,
Born on Monday.
Christened on Tuesday.
Married on Wednesday.
Took ill on Thursday.
Worse on Friday.
Died on Saturday.
Buried on Sunday.
That was the end
of Solomon Grundy.

b

c

3 Draw a 'Wednesday' card for Solomon Grundy.

Reading skills: *comprehension*
Writing skills: *planning, drafting*

Writing invitations

When we are having a special celebration we often invite others to join us. We send invitations to them.

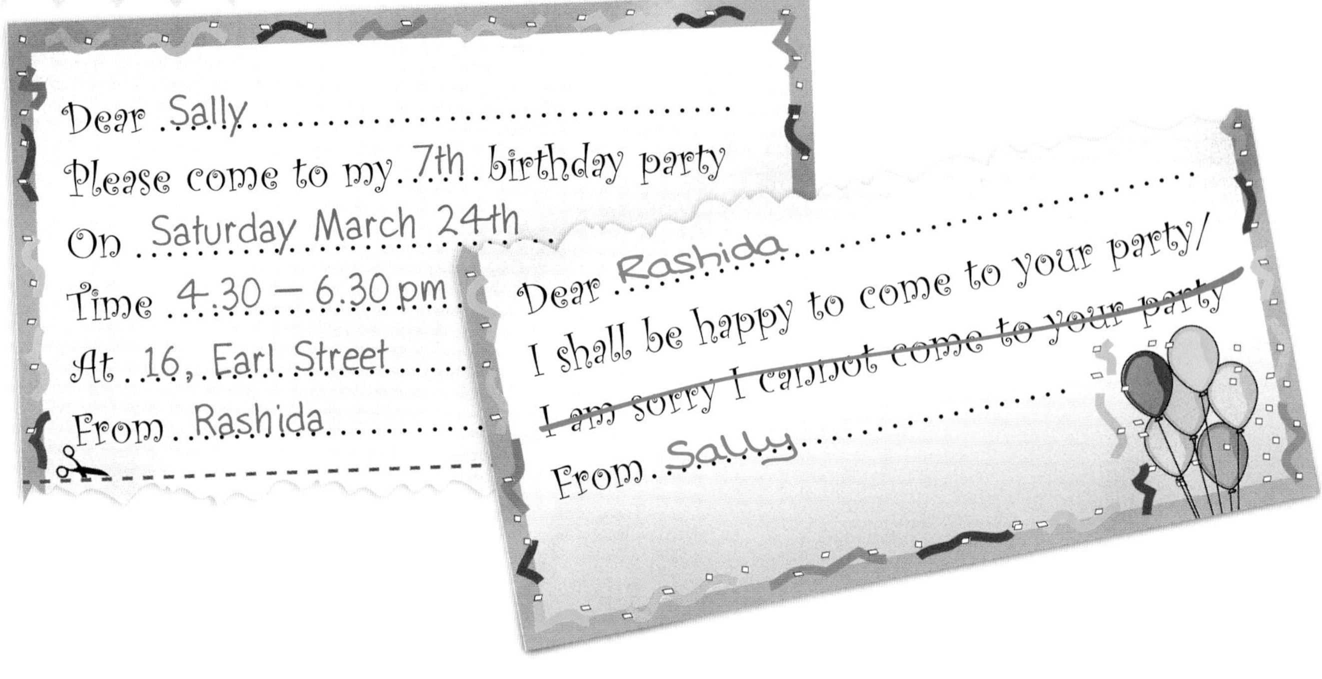

1 Answer these questions.

a Who is having a party?
b What is the party for?
c How old will Rashida be?
d Can Sally come?

Remember
Don't forget to put the date, time and place on the invitation.

2 Imagine your ideal party. Write an invitation to invite a friend. Remember to say when you are having the party, the time and where it will be.

Glossary
questions

Using adjectives

Rashida was given these presents for her birthday. Rashida could say: "I got a bracelet." **or** "I got a beautiful red, sparkling bracelet." 'beautiful', 'red' and 'sparkling' are all **adjectives**. They are words that describe what the bracelet was like.

1 Add adjectives to Rashida's **description** of her other presents.

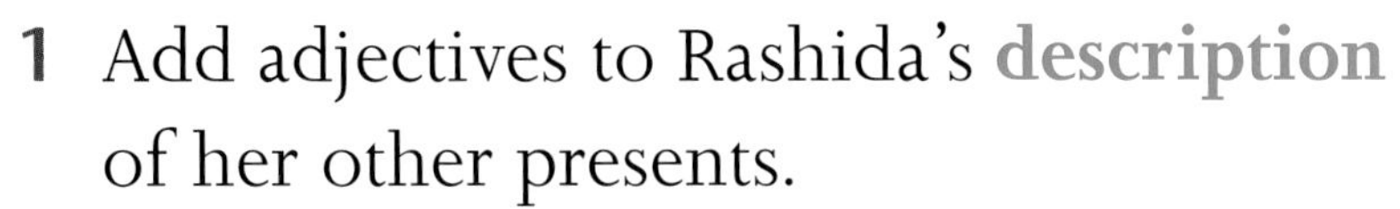

a I got a ______ ______ box of sweets.

b I also got ______ ______ books about cats.

2 Here are some more of Rashida's presents and adjectives that describe them. Write a **sentence** describing each present. In each sentence use the adjectives below and try to add one more adjective of your own.

a brown, cuddly

b round, black and white

c spotted, woollen

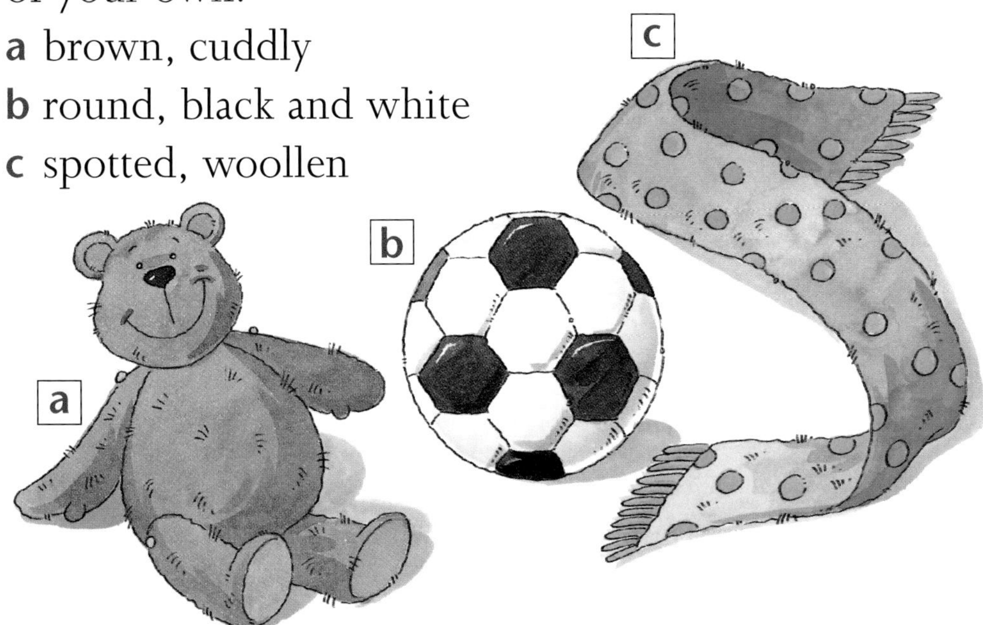

3 Imagine you are going to buy a present for Rashida. Describe what you would buy. Use adjectives to add detail to your description.

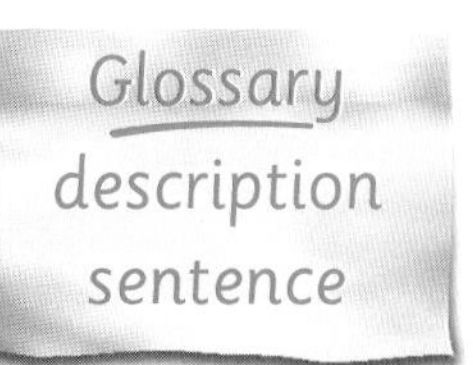

Adding detail

1 Here is a picture of Rashida's birthday cake. Write a description of the cake using lots of **adjectives** to add detail.

2 When you have written your description underline all the adjectives.

3 How many candles are there on Rashida's cake?

We say 'one candle' but 'seven candles'. 'Candles' is the **plural** of 'candle'. Plural means more than one. We add an 's' to many **nouns** to make them plural.

4 Write the plural of these words.

a balloon
b card
c drink
d streamer

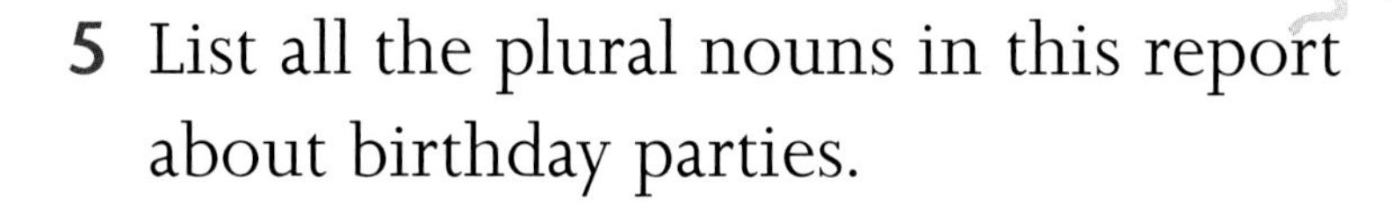

5 List all the plural nouns in this report about birthday parties.

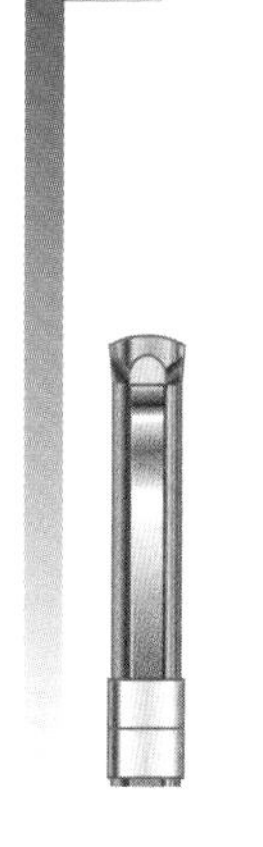

Birthday parties are held to celebrate the day someone was born. Friends and family come to the party. They bring presents and cards. They have lots of nice food like cakes, biscuits and crisps. Games are often played and prizes can be won.

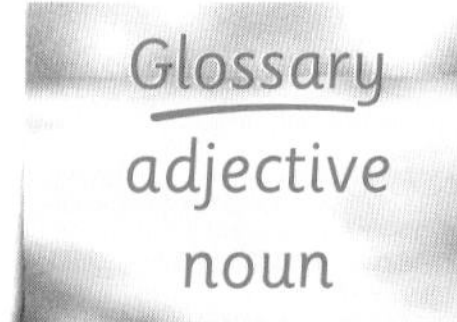

Writing skills: *description*

Reading skills: *alphabetical order*

Describing a game

1 These are the games that were played at Rashida's party. Choose one of the games and write a **description** of it and how it is played. The first sentence is started for you. Use the word lists to help you.

Party games
- musical chairs
- blind man's bluff
- pin the tail on the donkey

line of chairs
dance round
music stops
sit down

picture
donkey
blindfold
scarf

blindfold
turned round
catch someone
guess

1 Musical chairs is a game where you have to

Rashida had twelve friends at her party. Here are their names.

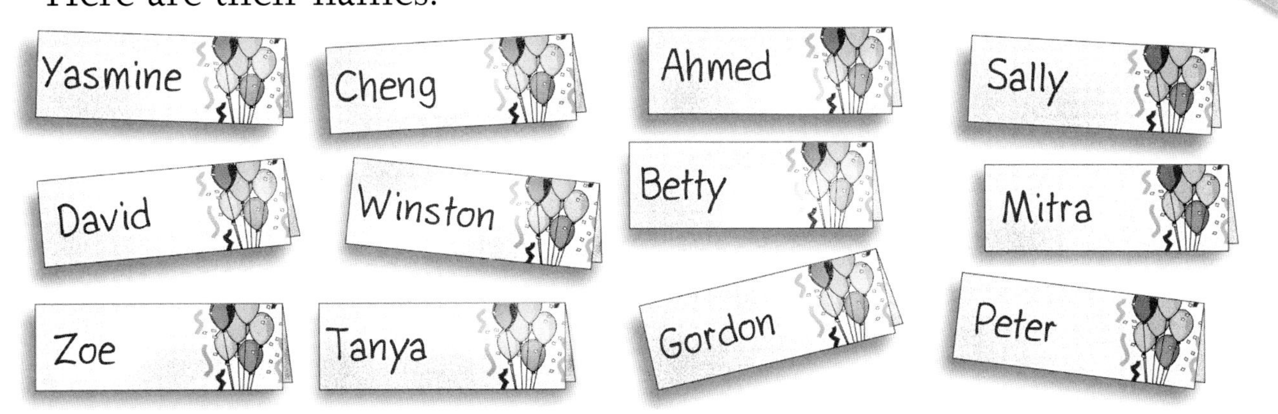

2 The children lined up in **alphabetical order** to play the games. List their names in the right order. Don't forget to put Rashida on the list.

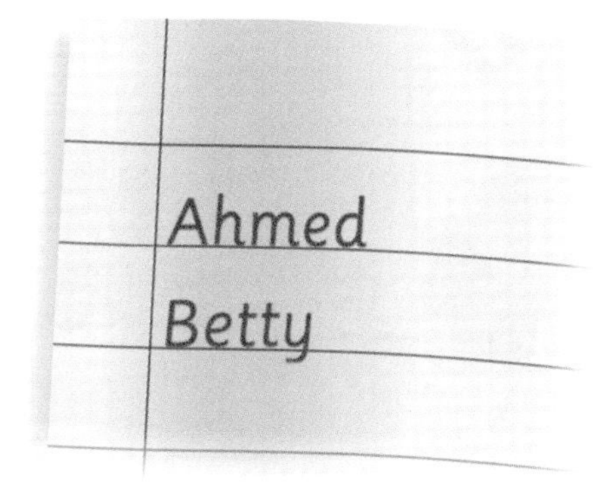

Glossary
description
alphabetical order

Using charts

Now we will look at another way of giving information about festivals – a chart.

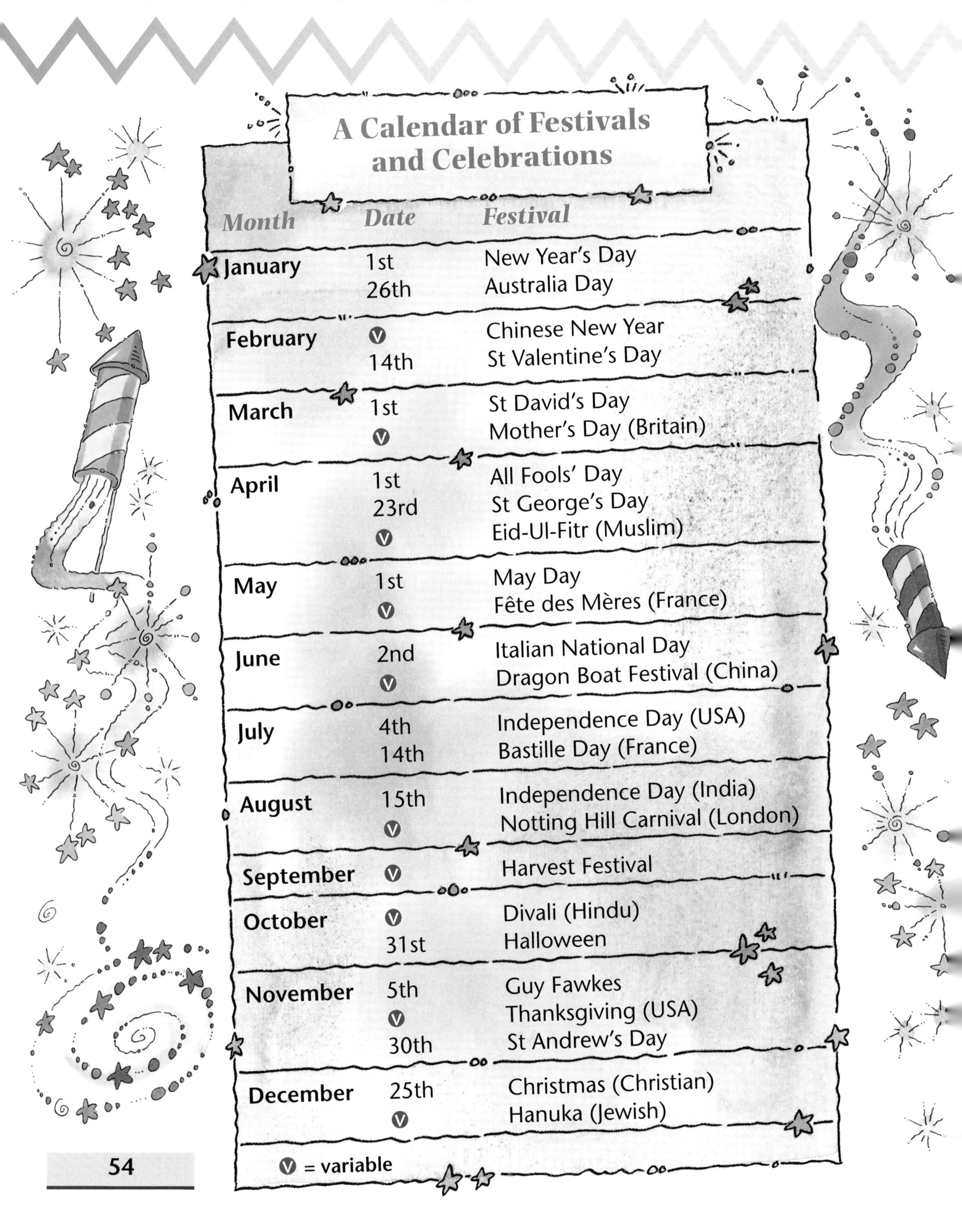

A Calendar of Festivals and Celebrations

Month	*Date*	*Festival*
January	1st 26th	New Year's Day Australia Day
February	Ⓥ 14th	Chinese New Year St Valentine's Day
March	1st Ⓥ	St David's Day Mother's Day (Britain)
April	1st 23rd Ⓥ	All Fools' Day St George's Day Eid-Ul-Fitr (Muslim)
May	1st Ⓥ	May Day Fête des Mères (France)
June	2nd Ⓥ	Italian National Day Dragon Boat Festival (China)
July	4th 14th	Independence Day (USA) Bastille Day (France)
August	15th Ⓥ	Independence Day (India) Notting Hill Carnival (London)
September	Ⓥ	Harvest Festival
October	Ⓥ 31st	Divali (Hindu) Halloween
November	5th Ⓥ 30th	Guy Fawkes Thanksgiving (USA) St Andrew's Day
December	25th Ⓥ	Christmas (Christian) Hanuka (Jewish)

Ⓥ = variable

Reading skills: *understanding a chart*

Vocabulary: *months of the year*

1 Look at the chart opposite and answer these **questions**.

a When is St Valentine's Day ?

b What does France celebrate in July ?

c Name two festivals that do not happen on the same date every year.

d Name a Jewish festival from the chart.

2 Fill in the missing month.

a Guy Fawkes' night is in ______.

b Mother's Day is in ______.

c Bastille Day is in ______.

d Notting Hill Carnival is in ______.

e My birthday is in ______.

A saint that it is special to a particular country is called a patron saint. St George is the patron saint of England. Scotland's patron saint is St Andrew and the patron saint of Wales is St David.

3 This famous painting shows part of the story of St George and the dragon. Write a **description** of the dragon using lots of **adjectives**.

4 Copy and fill in this chart about patron saints' days. Remember to look at the Calendar of Festivals and Celebrations to get the details on dates.

Name of patron saint	Country	Date

Glossary
question
description
adjective

UNIT 4 Writing to report

Grammar: *exclamations*

Reading skills: *visual comprehension*

Exclamation marks

Sentences which show a lot of feeling are called **exclamations**. They end with an **exclamation mark**. EXAMPLE: **Oh, good!**

1 What do these people say? Add an exclamation mark to the end of each sentence so that it is an exclamation.

2 Look at these cards and decide what they say.

a I know Card A is a ________ card because the picture shows ________.

b I know Card B is a ________ card because the picture shows ________.

3 Write a message to go inside each card and finish it with an exclamation mark.

Glossary
sentence

Commas in lists

If there is a **list** within a **sentence** we use **commas** to separate the list words.

EXAMPLE: At Rashida's party we had crisps, sandwiches, jelly, biscuits and birthday cake.

1 The lists in these sentences are missing their commas. Write out the sentences, putting commas in the right places.

Remember
Don't put a comma before 'and'.

On Bonfire Night we had rockets silver fountains and sparklers.

At Divali I wore a sari earrings and a bracelet.

There were roses bellflowers and lilies in my sister's wedding bouquet.

For Harvest Festival I took apples potatoes and baked beans to school.

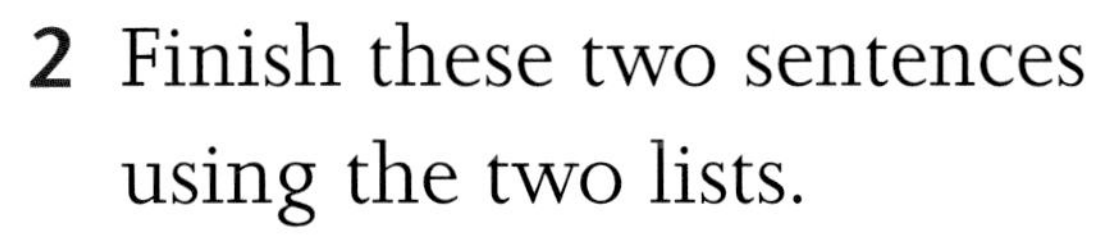

2 Finish these two sentences using the two lists.

a For Christmas I would like a computer game, ______, ______ and ______.

b I must remember to take my shorts, ______, ______ and ______.

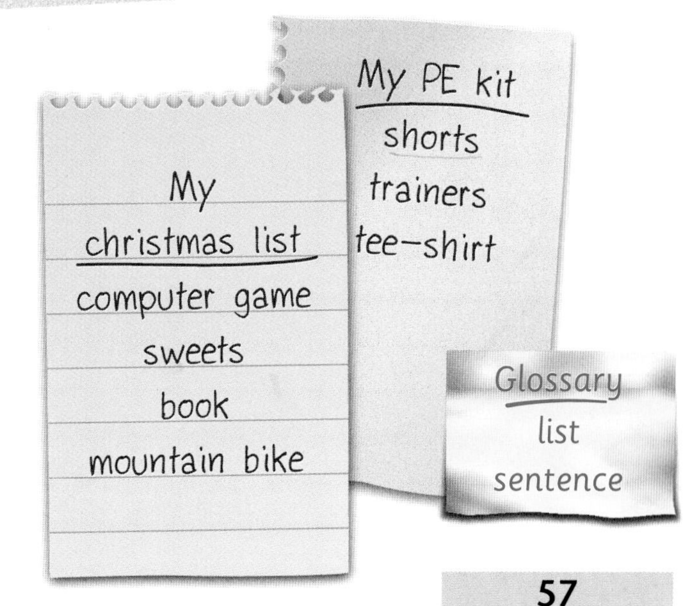

Glossary
list
sentence

Writing a report

Now you are going to write a report about a special day you like – it could be any of the different kinds of special days mentioned on pages 54 and 55.

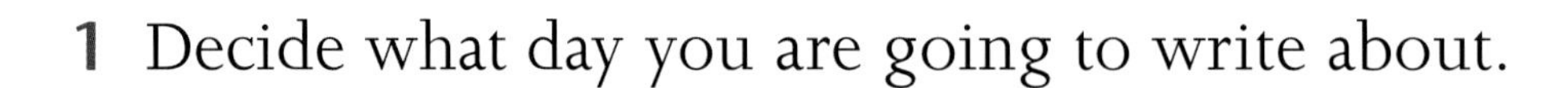

1 Decide what day you are going to write about.

2 Write what the day is by completing this sentence.

3 Brainstorm what special things happen on that day.

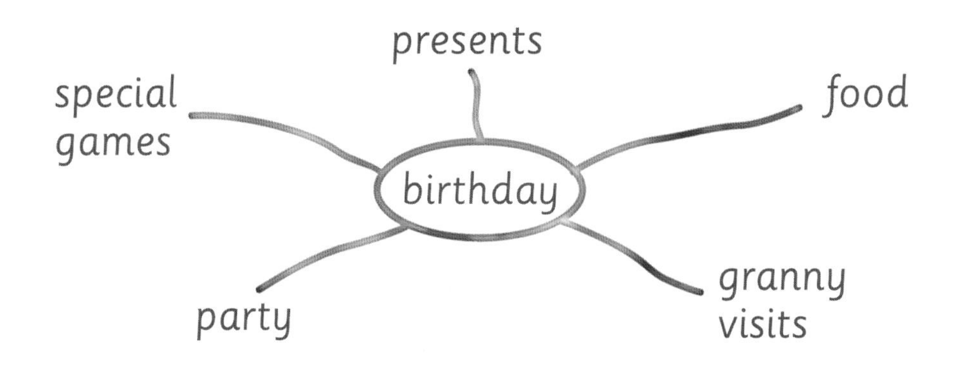

4 Add details to each special part of the day.

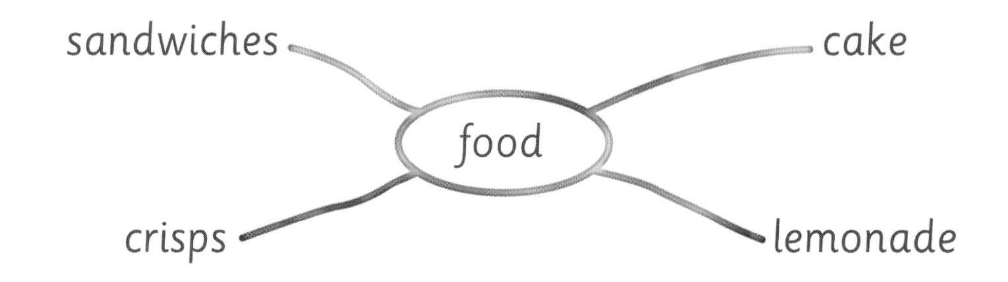

5 Complete these sentences using the notes you have made.

6 Add adjectives to your sentences so that they are good descriptions.

7 Use the sentence that you wrote for question 2 and the sentences you have just written to write the first draft of your report. You might decide to re-order the sentences or leave some out.

8 Swap your draft with a friend.
Discuss these questions.
- Is it clear?
- What extra detail could you add?
- Have you mentioned all the important things?

9 Make changes to your first draft using the ideas you and a friend have come up with.

10 Write out your report and decorate it with a festive border.

Glossary

adjective A word that goes with a noun and tells us about it.
EXAMPLE: a **blue** balloon

alphabet The letters in the alphabet are: abcdefghijklmnopqrstuvwxyz.

alphabetical order Words, phrases or sentences can be put in alphabetical order by putting the beginning letters in order.

author A person who writes books, stories, poems, etc.

brainstorm A way of writing down ideas when planning writing.

capital letter The capital letters are: ABCDEFGHIJKLMNOPQRSTUVWXYZ.

character A character is an individual in a story, play or poem. The things they do and say tell us what they are like.

chronological order/non-chronological Chronological order is the order in which events happen. Chronological writing is written in time order.
EXAMPLE: an account of a day that starts in the morning and goes through to the evening.
Non-chronological writing is not written in time order.

comma A punctuation mark used to break up sentences so that they are easier to understand. Commas are used to separate items in a list that is part of a sentence.
EXAMPLE: I bought eggs**,** fish and some chocolate.

command A sentence telling someone to do something.

consonant/vowel In the English alphabet there are 5 vowels (a e i o u) and 21 consonants (bcdfghjklmnpqrstvwxyz).

definition A statement giving the meaning of a word or phrase.

description Words which enable the reader/listener to form an idea of an object, event or feeling.

diagram A type of picture that explains something.

draft A piece of writing which is not in finished form.

edit To change the grammar, spelling, punctuation or words in writing before it is finished.

exclamation mark A punctuation mark used at the end of a sentence to indicate strong feelings. EXAMPLE: Help**!**

fiction
non-fiction Fiction is an invented story, poem or play.
Non-fiction is writing about real events, feelings or things.

full-stop A full-stop is a mark used to end a sentence when the sentence is not a question or exclamation.
EXAMPLE: The cat sat on the mat**.**

homographs Words that are spelt the same but have different meanings.
EXAMPLE: **swing**

homophones Words which sound the same but have different meanings and spelling. EXAMPLE: **been** and **bean**

imperative An imperative sentence commands or tells the reader or listener to do something. EXAMPLE: Run over there.

instructions Instructions tell us how to do something.

label The words which tell us about part of a diagram, picture or map.

list A group of things or names written down one after the other.

noun A word that names a person, feeling, thing or idea.

plan To work out what to say or write.

plural More than one.

poem A piece of writing which uses words and word order to create images and ideas. The lines often rhyme.

preposition A word telling us about the place of nouns or pronouns. EXAMPLES: on, under, in

punctuation A way of marking writing using full stops, capital letters, question marks etc. This helps the reader to understand.

question A sentence which needs a response. It ends with a question mark. EXAMPLE: What is your name?

question mark The punctuation mark at the end of a sentence.

report Reports describe things and detail their characteristics.

revise To make changes to a piece of writing to improve it.

rhyme Words which have the same ending sounds. EXAMPLES: man, pan.

rhyming couplet A pair of lines that rhyme.

rhythm The 'beats' in a piece of writing when it is read aloud.

sentence A sentence is a piece of language that can stand by itself and makes sense.

setting The time and place of events in a story.

simile A sentence or group of words which compares something to something else. EXAMPLE: As free as a bird.

speech marks The inverted commas that go around what is actually said in direct speech.
EXAMPLE: "I want my teddy," said the little boy.

tense Tense tells us when something is happening.
past tense Past tense: something has already happened.
EXAMPLE: I **sat** down. I **was sitting** down.
present tense Present tense: something is happening now.
EXAMPLE: She **is sitting** down. She **sits** down.

title The heading which tells us what writing is about.

verb A verb is a word that tells us what people are doing or being. EXAMPLE: The girl **ran** away.

verse A part of a poem.

	Genre focus	Range of texts	Text features	Reading skills
UNIT 1	Writing to instruct: instructions	instructions (things to make) instructions (things to do) directions (maps) diagrams dictionaries	aim materials and equipment steps in sequence diagrams labels lists	literal and inferential comprehension extracting information from maps and diagrams
UNIT 2	Writing to entertain: narrative	stories fiction and non-fiction	narrative opening character setting similes chronological order fiction/non-fiction illustrations diagrams	literal and inferential comprehension
UNIT 3	Writing to express: humorous poetry	poems limericks nursery rhymes rhyming couplets jokes	rhyme rhythm	literal and inferential comprehension
UNIT 4	Writing to inform: non-chronological reports	non-chronological report invitations descriptions charts	opening definition logically-ordered paragraphs photographs captions	literal and inferential comprehension extracting information from visual sources, maps and diagrams

Writing skills	Grammar	Punctuation	Words
writing sentences reading sentences sequencing labelling listing planning instructions drafting instructions revising instructions	sentences nouns prepositions verbs commands	capital letters full stops	alphabetical order labels technical words
writing sentences reading sentences similes planning a story drafting a story revising a story	sentences nouns adjectives verbs present tense past tense	speech marks	months seasons homophones
writing sentences reading sentences writing couplets writing limericks planning a poem drafting a poem revising a poem	sentences verbs 'a' or 'an' proper nouns	question marks capital letters	rhyming words vowels consonants question words onomatopeia contradictions homographs shortened words
writing sentences reading sentences descriptions planning a report drafting a report revising a report	sentences the verb 'to be' adjectives	exclamation marks commas in lists	days of the week singular and plural nouns alphabetical order months

OXFORD
UNIVERSITY PRESS

Great Clarendon Street, Oxford, OX2 6DP

Oxford New York
Athens Auckland Bangkok Bogotá Buenos Aires Calcutta
Cape Town Chennai Dar es Salaam Delhi Florence Honk Kong Istanbul
Karachi Kuala Lumpur Madrid Melbourne Mexico City Mumbai
Nairobi Paris São Paolo Singapore Taipei Tokyo Toronto Warsaw

and associated companies in Berlin Ibadan

First published 1999

British Library Cataloguing in Publication Data
Data available

Illustrated by: Lisa Berkshire, Teri Gower, Sophie Grillet, Nick Hawken, Alan Marks, Bethan Mathews, Shelagh McNicholas, Pat Moffett, Rhian Nest James, Wendy Sinclair, Merida Woodford

Photographs by: The Stock Market/Ariel Skelley (cover), /Chuck Savage (p47 bottom); Corbis UK Ltd/Kevin Fleming (p47 top), The National Gallery, London/Corbis (p55)

Acknowledgements
We are grateful for permission to reproduce the following copyright material in this book: Evelyn Beyer: 'Jump or Jiggle' from *Another Here and Now Story Book* by Lucy Sprague Mitchell, Copyright 1937 by E P Dutton renewed © 1965 by Lucy Sprague Mitchell, reproduced by permission of Dutton Children's Books, a division of Penguin Putman Inc; Denis Doyle: 'Shirley Said', first published in Apricot Rhymes by Dennis Doyle, reproduced by permission of the author; Colin McNaughton: 'There Was an Old Woman' from *Making Friends With Frankenstein: A Book of Monstrous Poems and Pictures*, Copyright © 1993 Colin McNaughton, reproduced by permission of the publisher, Walker Books Ltd., London; Judith Nicholls: 'Did You Really?', Copyright © 1998 reproduced by permission of the author; Libby Purves: extract from *The Hurricane Tree*, illustrated by P Lamont (Bodley Head), reproduced by permission of Random House UK Ltd; Marshmallow Treats recipe, reproduced by permission of Kelloggs Company.

We have made every effort to trace and contact copyright holders before publication. If notified, we will be pleased to rectify any errors or omissions where we have been unsuccessful.

ISBN 0 19 915549 6

Printed in Hong Kong